EDUCATION AND ADVANCEMENT

FOR THE

WORKING CLASSES.

A SPEECH

DELIVERED AT A PUBLIC MEETING AT

THE HACKNEY WORKING MEN'S INSTITUTE,

ON JANUARY 20TH, 1863.

By HARRY CHESTER,

CHAIRMAN OF THE COMMITTEE OF THE "METROPOLITAN ASSOCIATION FOR PROMOTING THE EDUCATION OF ADULTS" (IN UNION WITH THE SOCIETY OF ARTS).

———————————

LONDON:

BELL AND DALDY, 186, FLEET-STREET.

PRICE TWOPENCE.

EDUCATION AND ADVANCEMENT

FOR THE

WORKING CLASSES.

I HAVE come here this evening to talk to you about Education and
Advancement in Life—to explain how you may better your condition
through opportunities of education now offered to you. You know
that in all things an educated man has great advantages over an
ignorant man ; and that, whether you are mechanics, artizans, clerks,
labourers, or errand-boys, a good education, if your characters be
good, will help to lift you to posts of trust and skill, and therefore to
higher wages. A good education, even in the case of the poorest
child, includes long teaching and training ; for nothing less affords a
fair chance of being useful, good, and happy, and prepared for the
great realities of life here and hereafter. Time, then, is required for
the child's education ; but time is the poor child's difficulty.

Did it ever occur to you to consider, in reference to education,
what is the difference between a child and a puppy or a colt ? The
young horse or dog grows to its full size and strength in a few years
or months ; and may be educated, "broken in," in a short time ; so
that, when it is a few years old, it has all the sense and knowledge
that it can ever have. But you cannot treat children so. You
cannot "break in" a child as a young horse or dog. Our boys and
girls are a long while coming to maturity ; and there is no period in
their lives in which you can say of them, "They can learn no more."

Let us agree upon two points—Children must have a good education ; and it must be spread over a long time.

Fathers and mothers among the poorer classes, though anxious to
get the best schooling for their children, and willing to make
sacrifices for it, are seldom able to keep them at a day-school after
the age of 10 or 12. Little Tom or Mary must help to make the pot
boil, either by earning the small wages of childish labour, or by
assisting father or mother in their work. It is feared, too, that a
child not put early to work will never be handy at work at all.
There is great truth in this : but, nevertheless, I repeat that your
children must have a good education ; and that, to be good, it must
be spread over a long time. What is to be done ?

Let us inquire what the wealthier sort of people do with their
children, for, " what is sauce for the goose is sauce for the gander,"
all the world over ; and, as the human mind is essentially the same

in all classes of society, the same principles of education are applicable to rich and poor, though the modes of their application may be often necessarily different.

The rich man never dreams of cramming into the short period which ends at ten or twelve years of age the whole education of his children, as pellets of food are crammed down the throats of the geese at Strasburg. He keeps his daughter at school, or under governesses and teachers at home, till young miss is seventeen or eighteen years old; and his son, after working at school till that age, is sent to college, or the University, where he fags on at his books for three or four additional years. Why does the father incur this expense? and why does the son show this perseverance in his studies? Both the father and the son are aware that a complete education gives the best chance of success in life; and the University offers various advantages:—1st. A young man is not told vaguely to study. Definite courses of study, sufficiently various to suit various minds and tastes, are pointed out to him; and the books which he is to read are specified. 2nd. He is not left to find out for himself how he gets on in his studies. At stated periods he is examined by competent examiners. 3rd. He is not left to be his own trumpeter proclaiming his own attainments. The result of his examination (if he is successful) is not only proclaimed to the whole world by the University itself, but is embodied in a " Degree," which is in effect a certificate of his success, and a valuable testimonial in his favour. 4th. He has opportunities of competing with others of his own age and station, coming from all parts of the kingdom, for honours and substantial rewards, which not only commend him to notice but supply him with hard cash. 5th. Many valuable appointments are reserved for those who have taken these " Degrees."

You will say, " This is all very fine, but what is it to me? These good things are for the rich. There is nothing of this sort for me and mine." I came here to-night to tell you that there is something very like this for you and yours, if you will take advantage of it; and you shall hear something of a lad of nineteen, who, by taking advantage of it, has recently jumped from the receipt of 15s. a week, at Bradford, into the receipt of £1 18s. 7¼d. a week, in a Government office in London. Am I then going to pack you all off to Oxford and Cambridge, and to keep you for three years or more at the University? No; but I am going to explain to you how we have made a sort of an university for the working classes, and brought it with all its advantages to their very doors in all parts of the kingdom.

The two great International Exhibitions, in Hyde Park in 1851, and at South Kensington in 1862, were originated by a society, founded 109 years ago, and commonly called " The Society of Arts." Its full name is " The Society for the Encouragement of Arts, Manufactures, and Commerce." Not merely fine Arts, mind you, but industrial Arts as well; the noble " Arts" of shoemaking, tinkering, book-keeping, and bricklaying, just as much as the " Arts" of painting, modelling, and sculpture. The Exhibition of 1851 taught us many valuable lessons, and none more valuable than this, that, great as are our advantages as a nation, noble as is the character of our people, if the United Kingdom is to hold its own in the great competitions of industry with other countries, the education of our working classes must be improved. In the autumn of 1851 the Society of Arts set to work to stir up the country to provide better means and stronger motives for this improvement. Our first object was to extend the period of education, not by keeping children longer at their day schools, but by providing evening classes and evening schools, where, after leaving the day schools, children and persons no longer children in age, might continue their education without interfering with their daily bread-winning.

We formed a "Union of Institutions" for mutual encouragement and help. We invited into union with the Society of Arts the evening classes, mechanics' institutes, people's colleges, and similar bodies in all parts of the kingdom. We strengthened many and called many into existence. We procured an Act of Parliament to protect their property, and to enable them to manage their own affairs. We pointed out what such institutions should be and do: that they should provide amusement and refreshment; libraries whence books might be taken home to the family; reading-rooms supplied with instructive and amusing books and periodicals, and with newspapers keeping a man alive to all that goes on in the world; museums and occasional exhibitions to instruct his mind through his eyes; music and dramatic readings, which he might enjoy with his wife and family; games and exercises of skill, agility and strength; lectures for instruction and amusement; and, invariably, classes for systematic instruction.

But to keep these "Classes" on foot was the great difficulty of the Institutions, and, to enable them to overcome it by offering to the young men and women of the working classes some of those encouragements which a University offers to the young men of the wealthier classes, we established the system of Examinations, Certificates, and Prizes, which I will now explain to you.

The Society of Arts has appointed a Central Board of 29 Examiners, to examine candidates in 29 different subjects, all of which may be studied with advantage by the working classes. These examiners are gentlemen of the highest reputation, and are paid for their services. Each examiner (1) draws up a short notice to guide the reading of those who wish to be examined in his subject; (2) prepares his paper of questions to be answered in writing by the candidates; and (3) passes judgment upon the written answers. But the working classes are in all parts of the kingdom, and cannot go to the examiner, nor can the examiner split himself into fragments and go to them. Therefore, wherever there are candidates to be examined, a "Local Board of Examiners" is formed to co-operate with the Central Board. More than 100 of such Boards already exist, some in London, a few in Scotland and Ireland, and the greater part in the country towns of England; and additional Boards can be formed wherever they may be requisite to bring the examinations, certificates, and prizes within easy reach of the working classes. The duties of the Local Boards are of two kinds, because the examinations are of two kinds. There are Preparatory Examinations and Final Examinations, and no one can undergo the latter without first undergoing one of the former.

The Local Boards hold the former and superintend the local working of the latter.

There are three kinds of preparatory examination; one very simple and easy; one simple and easy, but not quite so much so as the first; and one intended merely to sift the candidates who wish to undergo the final examinations.

If, being 16, you can read, write, spell, and do common sums in arithmetic, and if you have reason to think that you can pass a satisfactory examination for a certificate or prize in the final examinations, all that you have to do is to satisfy the Local Board that you have these qualifications, and they will give you a " *Pass*," admitting you to the final examinations.

If, however, you are under 16, or, being 16, your education has been so neglected that you cannot read, write, spell, and do common sums satisfactorily, or if your knowledge of none of the 29 advanced subjects is such as to make it likely that you will obtain a certificate in the final examination, then you should prepare for, and undergo, one of the two simple elementary examinations, which the Local Board holds, as a preparation for the higher examination. Make a " trial trip" with the Local Board before you start with ths Central Board. You may obtain from the Local Board, if you are successful in their elementary examination, a certificate or a prize, but not, of course, of so high a value as those awarded in the final examinations. Both kinds of certificate, however, are current all over the kingdom; because those issued by the Society of Arts itself, on the award of its Central Board, are perfectly uniform; and those issued by the Local Boards on their own authority, vary only in the local titles of the Boards, and purport to be issued by Boards in Union with the Society of Arts. The preparatory examinations will be held everywhere, in 1863, in the evenings of the 3rd, 4th, 5th, and 6th of March; and the final examinations everywhere in the evenings of the 5th, 6th, 7th, and 8th of May. The candidates are assembled in quiet rooms, in their own neighbourhoods, with none present but themselves and a few members of the Local Board, who are there to keep order and to see fair play. The candidates are seated; the printed papers are put before them; pen, ink, and paper are supplied; there is plenty of time for every one to write the answers. The answers, as soon as written, are sealed up and sent to the examiners. They know the candidates only by numbers, not by their names. The certificates are awarded for positive merit, not for comparative merit. If you get a sufficient number of marks to entitle you to a certificate, you will receive it without the least reference to any other candidate's having got a greater number of marks than you. The prizes are given to those who obtain the greatest number of marks, provided that they are not teachers, nor pupil-teachers, nor persons belonging to the higher classes of society. The examinations were established for the good of the working classes, and they alone can compete for the prizes. I cannot tell you what prizes are given in the preparatory examinations, because those prizes are given by the Local Boards (with help from the Metropolitan Association for Promoting the Education of Adults) and vary in various places. In the final examinations there are at least two prizes, one of £5 and one of £8, at the disposal of each of the twenty-nine examiners; in some of the subjects there are additional prizes given by members of the Society of Arts; and there is also the "Prince Consort's Prize." He was President of the Society of Arts, and I will tell you what is meant by the "Prince Consort's Prize."

It has been commonly the fate of princes to be flattered in life and abused at death, but very different has been the fate of our great and good Prince Albert. Such a character as his—so grand and simple—could not be generally appreciated while he lived; but ever since he was taken from us, it has risen day by day; and, as it becomes more and more known and understood, it will continue to rise higher and higher. No other prince or great personage that I have heard of has walked so wisely, loftily, and loyally in the path of most difficult duty as this prince. He took a warm interest in our examinations. He minutely considered all the details of the plan, and improved them by his admirable judgment. Very wise and liberal he was in his opinions, very reliant on the good sense and good feeling of the people. I remember, when we proposed, at one time, to offer higher prizes in some of the twenty-nine subjects of examination than in others, he asked "Why this difference?" It was answered, "Because, sir, we think that some of these subjects are better suited than others to working men." He said, "I think you had better make no difference. The working men themselves are the best judges of what will suit them. They will find out what is most useful to them." At another time his Royal Highness was desirous to facilitate the carrying out of a plan which would have given a most valuable extension to the examinations, and, through them, to the industrial instruction of the people; and he expressed his intention (if the plan were adopted) to give medals, stamped with his own portrait, to all the candidates who obtained certificates of the 1st class. How I wish that the plan had been carried out; and that many thousands of you, my friends, were now in possession of such medals, treasured memorials not only of your own success in the examinations, but of the sympathy and approval of that great and good man!

A few months before his death, thinking that those working men and women who had obtained certificates should have some continued encouragement to persevere in their efforts for self-improvement, the Prince announced his intention to give annually a prize of twenty-five guineas, to be called "The Prince Consort's Prize," to the candidate who should gain the greatest number of certificates of the first-class in each period of four years. Long before this prize could be awarded, the nation was called upon to mourn his loss. But the prize was not allowed to drop. The Queen, in her sorrow—

heavier, I verily believe, than ever before fell to the lot of a loving wife—for what other woman ever had such weighty duties and responsibilities as hers, or received such constant, loving, wise, un-selfish loyal help as she received from him?—the Queen, determining to carry on as far as possible his good works, remembered, you may be sure, this prize offered to the working classes; and she continues it in his name. This, then, the Prince's legacy and the Queen's gift, is "the Prince Consort's Prize," which every one of yourselves, with good natural abilities and perseverance in self-improvement, has year after year an opportunity of gaining.

It was gained in May, 1862, by a young lad of 19, employed at 15s. a week in a merchant's house, at Bradford, in Yorkshire. He was a warehouseman's son. He was at school four years, and left it when he was 12 years of age. He connected himself with the Bradford Mechanics' Institution. He first presented himself for examination at Bradford, in 1859, when he was 16. He took up arithmetic and algebra, and gained a certificate of the first class in arithmetic and one of the second class in algebra. In 1860 he gained two certificates of the first class in English history and in geography. In 1861 he gained four certificates,—in English literature first; in algebra second; in geometry second; and in trigonometry third. In 1862 he gained three certificates,—in algebra a first; in trigonometry a second; and in geometry a first, with the first prize of £5—that is to say, in the whole competition of candidates in geometry he was first of all. Mark his perseverance. In algebra he got the lowest certificate in 1859, the second certificate in 1861, the first in 1862. In geometry he got a certificate of the second class in 1861, a first class and the highest prize in 1862. In trigonometry he got a third class in 1861, and second class in 1862. These certificates entitled him to the highest honour that the Society of Arts can bestow on a candidate in the examinations; that is to say, "The Prince Consort's Prize" of twenty-five guineas, given by her Majesty the Queen. The prize, with a special certificate, setting forth its character and origin, was presented to him publicly by Sir Thomas Phillips, the Chairman of the Council of the Society of Arts, at the opening of the Society's 109th Session in November last. Whether he will reappear in the examinations I cannot say, for he is now a clerk in the Privy Council Office. The late Mr. John Wood, Earl Granville, the Earl of Derby, and Viscount Palmerston, have occasionally allowed the Society of Arts to nominate young men who have done best in the examinations to compete with others for appointments in the public service. Last autumn Lord Granville very kindly allowed the "Prince Consort's Prizeman" to enter into one of these competitions. He succeeded; and passed at a jump from his 15s. a week at Bradford to £1 18s. 7½d. a week (or £100 a year, increasing to a maximum of £300 a year), in the department of the Committee of Privy Council on Education. Time runs fast; but I must tell you another case. The son of a working jeweller in London joined the Metropolitan Evening Classes, now the City of London College; when he was 16 he presented himself for examination; and having gained several certificates, his friends saw his abilities to be more than common, and were desirous that he should be enabled to follow the bent of his own inclination, which was to make the law his profession. His father was unable to maintain him and to provide him with the requisite books. Lord Stanley, Secretary of State for India, advertised for young fellows of good character to compete for certain clerkships in his office. Encouraged by his success in our examinations, our young fellow competed for and gained a clerkship. That enabled him to maintain himself, working in his office by day and at his law by night. An Act of Parliament having combined the two Indian establishments in Leadenhall-street and in Cannon-row, a considerable reduction of the clerks was determined on. Some were selected to retire, with a compensation for the loss of their appointments. He was not one of them; but he obtained permission to retire with a small compensation in place of one of those who had been selected for retirement, but desired to stay. On this compensation money my young friend lived while it lasted; and, when it was spent, we represented his case to the Governors of the "Tancred Scholarships," and they were so satisfied with his merits that they made him a "Tancred Scholar," and thus enabled him to maintain himself in the study of the law until he can be called to the bar. I think we shall all hear of him again under circumstances which will warrant his next biographer in giving him a longer notice.

Five hundred of the largest employers of labour have signed a declaration approving of the examination, and recognising the certificates as trustworthy testimonials.

It is not, however, chiefly as testimonials that I value the certificates. Good for what they say of you to others, they are far better for what they say of you to yourselves. They assure you of the extent and value of your knowledge, and it is a great thing to be sure that you have a sound knowledge of any subject.

Burns, the Scotch poet, a very poor working man, says—

> Oh ! wad some power the giftie gie us
> To see ourselves as others see us,
> It wad frae monie a blunder free us,
>   And foolish notion.

When we have been fagging hard at the study of any subject we are very apt to fall into one of these two opposite "blunders;" either we "see ourselves" in the light of vanity, as very wonderful folk, or we "see ourselves" with self-disparaging eyes, undervaluing our acquirements, and therefore neither turning them to account by using them, nor taking encouragement to improve them. But when competent examiners "see us," i.e., our acquirements, and award to us certificates of the 1st, 2nd, or 3rd class, or even a prize, or (on the other hand) nothing but a ": Pluck," we "see ourselves as others see us," and we form a just notion of ourselves.

I think it very right and useful that advancement in life, valuable appointments, higher wages, more power and influence, should be looked for, in a moderate spirit, as direct results of superior education. Among the wealthier classes, there is generally a desire to "get on," to turn acquirements to account in the great struggles of life. If this were not so, we should lose a great natural motive—not the highest, but a natural and honest motive—to self-improvement, and we should have stagnation where there ought to be a constant advance. This being true of the wealthy classes, I think it is even more true of the poor; and I should be very sorry to see you too dull and indifferent to be thus moved. But, "What about contentment?" I think I hear some one ask. Well, it is right, and our duty to be contented in our station. I advise you to make the best of your lot, to put away gloominess and grumbling, and to cultivate a cheerful, happy spirit. But no law, human or divine, bids us to be so contented with our station as to make no attempts to improve it by the use of such talents as we have received from God. His gifts may safely be used, and cultivated to the best of our power; and if, using all honesty and no mean practices, and not being over anxious to rise, we see before us natural opportunities of rising, we may use them with a good conscience, and hope to do more good to the world than we could have done in a lower station.

In this country, happily, a man with good abilities and character may rise from the lowest to the highest class, and leave behind him memories which his countrymen will not willingly let die. You all know the cases of the Stephensons, George and Robert—of the Peels and Arkwrights. Do you know that his Grace the Lord Archbishop of York, who is the third person in the kingdom after the Royal family, was once a little boy in a National school? Lord Tenterden (the eminent judge), and Turner (the great painter, whose grand pictures you see at South Kensington) were the sons of barbers; Telford (the famous engineer), Ben Jonson (the rare poet, whose epitaph, "Oh, rare Ben Jonson," you see in Westminster Abbey), and Hugh Miller were masons; Inigo Jones (the architect of Whitehall Chapel) and John Hunter (who discovered the circulation of the blood in our veins) were carpenters; Cardinal Wolsey and Defoe were sons of butchers; John Bunyan (who wrote "The Pilgrim's Progress") was a tinker; Herschel was a bandsman; Etty (the painter) was a printer; Sir Thomas Lawrence (who painted portraits of kings, queens, emperors, statesmen, generals, and other bigwigs) was the son of a tavern-keeper; the illustrious James Watt was the son of an instrument maker; Michael Farraday is the son of a blacksmith; Sir Isaac Newton's father was a yeoman, having a small farm, worth about 11s. 6½d. a week; Milton was the son of a scrivener; Pope and Southey were sons of linendrapers; Sir Humphry Davy was apprentice to a country apothecary; Shakspeare was the son of a butcher and grazier; Lord Eldon (the celebrated Lord Chancellor) was the son of a Newcastle coalfitter; Lord St. Leonards (who was Lord Chancellor ten years ago) is the son of a barber, and began life as an errand boy. Honour to all these worthies! Double honour to them, say I, because of the difficulties of their origin. You will find all this, and much more, in Smiles's "Self Help." But all these were remarkable men; and few can hope to become as great as they. You cannot all rise out of your own natural class to become archbishops and lords chancellor, and to leave behind you famous memories, of which our country shall be always proud. True; but some of you may do even this; and if in times past, when there existed no special system for the discovery of talent in poor boys, so many of them made their way up to high places, what may you not expect in future, now that such a system does exist; now that in every corner of the kingdom a lad may undergo examination and make his talent to be known? Every one of you, by training his mind, acquiring knowledge, and having a good character, may raise himself, if not above his class, very notably in his class; and by so raising himself may help to raise the level of his whole class. These are worthy objects of ambition; but, after all, the grandest object is the reward which a man finds in himself, viz., increased powers of understanding and doing. We think it a great folly and a great sin for a man to starve his body, that body which His Creator gave him to nourish, develope, and train to its various wonderful uses. Is it less a folly and a sin to starve the mind, which was given to him by his Creator to be nourished with knowledge, developed by exercise, and trained to its still more wonderful uses?

Let me beg of you then not to neglect the advantages now offered to you. Remember that they are offered to your whole class throughout the kingdom; and that if you—in London—avail yourselves of them less readily than your fellows in other places, you will be worse off than before, because they will get before you and leave you behind. Nor is this all:—Think of other countries—Paris is now within ten hours and a half from London; and Paris swarms with evening schools for the working classes. If the French artisan, or the Belgian artisan, is to be better educated than his rival in England, the latter will be beaten in the markets of the world. Don't let us delude ourselves. There is no branch of industry whatever in which well-educated workmen will not surpass ignorant workmen. If we neglect to place within the reach of the people the best possible education, or if the people neglect to use it to the greatest possible extent, we shall certainly drift behind other nations in the world-wide competitions of manufactures, and—when this happens—you know what follows:—Selling at a loss, diminution of manufacture, half-time, lowering of wages, discharge of hands, want of wages, pawning and selling of goods, insufficiency of food, warmth, and clothing, premature removal of children from school, loss of health, and strength, and energy, national decay, and wretchedness of all kinds.

The working classes of London, in proportion to their numbers, have not hitherto profited by our examinations, certificates, and prizes, as fully as the same classes at Glasgow, Leeds, Bradford, Devonport, and other places, and this is one of the reasons why we have formed the "Metropolitan Association for Promoting the Education of Adults" among you.

We are engaged in establishing in all parts of London "Local Boards" in connexion with the Society of Arts, that you may have easy access to the examinations, and in promoting the establishment of evening classes and evening schools, where you and your children may receive suitable instruction.

We propose also to encourage by certificates and prizes the industrial instruction of young women and girls, to qualify them to take respectable places in service, or to manage with skill and economy their father's or husband's homes; to encourage lads and girls, from 12 to 16, in the use of "drill" or other suitable exercises fitted to increase their activity, shapeliness, strength, and health; and further to do what we can for your recreation and amusement in time of leisure.

These are important objects. Will you co-operate with us in carrying them out?

A word to those who have children. As soon as they are old enough to go to school, put them to the best school in your neighbourhood, interest yourself in a regular manner in what they do at school, and let them understand that you expect them to do their best. I need not say set them a good example in all things, and pray for them habitually. Be sure you make them attend school very regularly. You little think how much they lose by irregular attendance. It is only the children of the poor who are irregular in their attendance at school, and these are just the children who ought to attend most regularly, because they have the least time to spend at school, and can least afford to waste it. Try hard to keep them at school till they are 12 years old, and then, if you send them to work, let me beg of you to make arrangements for their attendance, at least two or three times a week, at an evening school. As soon as they are 12 let them be presented at the preparatory examinations, which I have spoken of as suitable for children of that age. They will thus be encouraged and helped on to succeed in the greater examinations at 16. So much for children; now for persons 16 years old and upwards.

If your own education has been much neglected, I advise you to begin with the easiest preparatory examinations, and to work your way up to the higher ones. Don't be discouraged if you do not succeed at once. If you fail at first, don't throw the blame of your failure upon others. Take it like a man, and go at it again until you succeed. You certainly will succeed if you persevere. No one needs to be ashamed of being a poor scholar if he has had no opportunity of becoming a good scholar; but now such an opportunity is offered to every one, and you may be sure that, if fools laugh at the sight of age pursuing the studies which are more natural to youth, all those whose opinions are worth the quarter of a straw, will honour the man or woman who attends the evening school or class to make up for lost time. I cannot express to you with what pleasure and respect I have looked upon grown-up men and women, sometimes greyheaded ones, fagging away at their books, or at their pothooks and hangers, after perhaps a hard day's work. As to the subjects of examination, don't try too many at once. You cannot be examined in more than four of the twenty-nine advanced subjects in one year. Lay a first-rate foundation with plenty of the compo of reading, writing, and arithmetic. If you are not well grounded in them, you will do little good in anything else. Then look over the list of subjects and select the one which is most likely to suit you, and determine to understand it well—to master it. Ever so many smatterings of ever so many subjects will never place a certificate in your hands, nor be of much use to you; but a good solid bit of real knowledge of one subject, whatever it be, may give you not only a certificate but a prize; and the steady hard work by which you master your subject will prove a lasting good to your mind, exercising it, training it, and strengthening it, so that you will be twice the man that you were before, and find it much easier and pleasanter to acquire knowledge.

You will probably think it prudent to begin with some subject useful in your daily bread-winning; but I hope you will go on to master subjects which may improve you not only as a workman, but as a man and an English citizen, whose whole time and thoughts are not engrossed in winning the bread of daily life. If you are an assistant in a shop, or a clerk in a mercantile house, you can begin with "arithmetic" or "book-keeping;" and, if the firm have French or German correspondents, the "French" or "German" language will of course be useful to you. Ground yourself well in English grammar and composition, and take pains with your writing. If you are a mechanic, take the "principles of mechanics" or "practical mechanics." If a gardener, take "botany" in relation to gardening, and then "Latin." If a printer, or employed in a museum, or in a chemist's or apothecary's laboratory or shop, take "Latin;" or, in the two latter cases, take "chemistry." If you are a miner, take "mining and metallurgy." If you are engaged in any of the constructive trades, take "drawing." Indeed, everyone ought to be able to draw. "Music," which charms and refines, ought to be in every house. Every Englishman should be acquainted with "English history" and "English literature," and with the unerring laws of true "political economy" and "physiology in relation to health." In the list of subjects you will find "domestic economy;" and if you have a wife, daughter, sister, or sweetheart, I hope you will advise her to prepare for examination in that subject. A woman who had received a certificate in "domestic economy," with a sweet temper and a pious mind, and no nonsense, would be a treasure to a working-man, saving him from many of the evils which too commonly make his home wretched, and drive him to the public-house. She would know how to market, to make a little go a good way, to keep the house or the room and the children tidy, to cook a cheap bit of meat which should be palatable and strengthening, to tend the baby, nurse the sick, wash and mend the clothes, darn the stockings, and keep the buttons on the shirt. In her hands "the way the money goes" would be the right way, and it would not go too fast. You little think how much more comfort you could get out of your wages if your wife and you had some book-learning on these subjects. The book-learning would be of little use without practice; but what was learnt in the book should be practised in the home, and you would find your advantage in it. As for you younger fellows, who are not yet half yourselves, because you have not yet found your better halves, a word to you. When the time comes, as come it will if you are the hearty fellows I take you for, when you feel very tender about a certain pair of bright cheeks or black eyes, you must not trifle with the girl who owns them; but you need not be in a hurry to commit yourself until you know whether she has the necessary knowledge for managing the home and the babies. Just turn the talk upon the Society of Arts and its examinations in domestic economy, and find out whether she has a certificate; and, if she has none, you may quietly hint that you mean to marry a girl with a certificate. On the other hand, I give similar advice to the girls. Don't marry an ignoramus. When that good-looking young fellow, with whom you think it would be so pleasant to be classed in the parson's books for the rest of your life, plucks up his courage to examine you as to that most delicate matter, the state of your heart towards him, don't at once give him a certificate of your affection signed and sealed; but get father or mother to examine him as to the certificates which he has received, and let him understand that you are not going to marry one who knows little or nothing. An educated husband must not have an ignorant wife, nor an educated wife have an ignorant husband.

Our Association is very desirous to do something towards providing you with healthy amusements out of doors, and with suitable recreation and comfort in-doors.

When we speak of education, we mean not only book-learning and the discipline of the mind, but the training of the body also, and, in short, the *bringing out* of the whole man. Human beings are educated for good or evil by all the circumstances that surround them, not only in their schools but at their homes, their workshops, their amusements. Much has been done from this point of view for the working-classes of late years, but very much more remains to be done. Good examples to us Londoners have been set at Ipswich, Derby, Southampton, and other towns. I will tell you what they have done lately at Southampton. They have established a good kind of Mechanics' Institute, which they call a "Workman's Hall." It provides all the advantages that a good Institute provides, viz., books, newspapers, class-rooms for instruction, games, readings, recitations, singing, and cheap refreshments. Smoking is allowed. Very few of the institutes provide refreshments, but they should always be provided as they are at the Workman's Halls at Southampton. The three halls are governed by a council common to all, which is composed partly of working men, and by three executive committees, which are composed entirely of working men. The rooms are open on Sundays after two in the afternoon. All gambling and betting, and the use of intoxicating drinks, are excluded. On Sundays no books and periodicals but such as are considered suitable to the day are available. Assuming that this limitation is not construed too strictly, nor enforced in a sectarian spirit, the plan appears to me to be excellent. If, as every one admits, the institute is a good substitute for the public house as a resort for the working man on a week day, surely it must be still more so on a Sunday. They who have homes and families are not likely to spend a large part of their Sunday at the hall or institute; but how many there are who have neither family nor home! They cannot be all the afternoon and evening at church. Why should they not use their own halls on a Sunday as gentlemen without families and homes in London use their comfortable clubs?

The entire exclusion of drinks which may intoxicate is a difficult question. No one can have a greater horror of intemperance than I have; and if I thought that at these halls the working men could not have their glass of beer without abusing themselves to drunkenness, I should say, "Exclude beer absolutely." But my belief is the reverse of this. I know that the working classes have made great advances in temperance, and I believe that, to make them as temperate as the wealthier classes have become, we want only the same means of reformation as the wealthier classes have had, *i.e.*, not compulsory abstinence from all drinks capable of intoxicating, but improved and extended education, and places of recreation and amusement free from all temptations to drink to excess. Before gentlemen had their clubs, where no one has any pecuniary interest in the sale of drink, gentlemen frequented taverns, and were drunken. Give to the working men their institutes, clubs, or halls, and I believe that they will become as temperate as the gentlemen. All the surrounding circumstances will be in favour of temperance. The halls will be frequented by poor men, perhaps by rough men, but not by degraded men. The public opinion of the place will be against drunkenness; the committee will have the strongest motives to prevent it; no one will have any interest in promoting it, and I believe that these poor men's clubs will prove as valuable schools of temperance as the rich men's clubs have proved. Let us never forget that voluntary temperance is better than enforced abstinence. The latter is Jewish, the former Christian. But temperance is necessary, and, if it cannot be had without abstinence, abstinence must be enforced; but I think the question of enforcing it may safely be left to the decision of the working men themselves in each separate case.

One word more, and I have done. Among the twenty-nine subjects in which the Society of Arts gives certificates and prizes, there is no mention of religious knowledge. This is not because the Society of Arts is indifferent to religion, but because it is not within its province to inquire into that subject. No knowledge, however, can be half so important as religious knowledge; and, while it concerns a man much to know the extent and value of his knowledge in any branch of secular literature and science, it concerns him very much more to know how far his knowledge of religion is full and correct—or the reverse. "The Metropolitan Association for Promoting the Education of Adults" has therefore asked the Bishops of London and Winchester—and they have kindly consented—to appoint their own examiners to examine and give certificates to any candidates who may be willing to be examined by those examiners in the Bible and Prayer-book. These examinations are of course quite voluntary. The whole system is voluntary; but members of the Church of England will probably be glad to have their children, if not themselves, examined by the Bishop's examiners in the Creed, the Lord's Prayer, and other things which a Christian ought to know and believe.

'Though the whole of the certificates granted by the Society of Arts, the Metropolitan Associations, the Local Boards, and the Examiners appointed by the Bishops, are professedly certificates of attainment, not of character, I regard them as, indirectly, very valuable certificates of character. They do not fall to the idle, the frivolous, the dissipated, the drunken, but are evidences of energy, patience, perseverance, temperance, steadiness, and self-control. I regret that I have detained you so long, but the subjects of your education, and advancement through education, are so deeply interesting to me, that once set a-going upon them, like a clock wound up, I am apt to run down.

When I see poor children of ten or twelve years of age taken from their schools and sent into the world, as if their education were completed, when, in truth, it is just begun, it seems to me as sad as if, in this cold winter's night, they were sent into the streets without shoes and stockings, and with no covering but a handful of rags; and when I see a man or a woman unable to read and write, I feel pained as if I saw that the poor creatures were maimed, or blind, or dumb.

The Society of Arts, and the Metropolitan Association, now offer to you priceless advantages ; and for the sakes of yourselves and your children I heartily hope that you will use your very best endeavours to profit by the means of education and advancement which, as fellow men and fellow Christians, we place within your reach.

Any person who wishes to be examined, or to form a Local Board for the Examinations, or otherwise to assist in carrying them out, may obtain gratis from the Secretary of the " Society of Arts," John-street, Adelphi, or from Mr. Sales, the Secretary of the "Metropolitan Association for Promoting the Education of Adults," No. 19, John-street, Adelphi, W.C., or 9, Livermere-place, Dalston, N.E., Programmes and Papers containing all the requisite information.